GRAY FOXES, RATTLESNAKES,

AND OTHER MYSTERIOUS ANIMALS OF THE

EXTREME DESERTS

ANA MARÍA RODRÍGUEZ

Enslow Publishers, Inc.
40 Industrial Road
Box 398
Berkeley Heights, NJ 07922
USA

http://www.enslow.com

For my husband and sons, who share my journeys through extreme worlds

Acknowledgments

The author expresses her immense gratitude to the scientists who so kindly gave their time to comment on the manuscript and provided images to illustrate the book. Your help has been extremely invaluable.

Library of Congress Cataloging-in-Publication Data

Rodríguez, Ana María, 1958–.
 Gray foxes, rattlesnakes, and other mysterious animals of the extreme deserts / Ana María Rodríguez.
    p. cm. — (Extreme animals in extreme environments)
 Includes bibliographical references and index.
 Summary: "Explains why the world's deserts are extreme environments and examines how gray foxes, rattlesnakes, and other animals have adapted to the harsh climates"—Provided by publisher.
 ISBN 978-0-7660-3697-0
 1. Desert animals—Juvenile literature. 2. Deserts—Juvenile literature. I. Title.
 QL116.R63 2011
 591.754—dc22

                    2010015679

Paperback ISBN 978-1-4644-0020-9
ePUB ISBN 978-1-4645-0465-5
PDF ISBN 978-1-4646-0465-2

Printed in the United States of America

092011 Lake Book Manufacturing, Inc., Melrose Park, IL

10 9 8 7 6 5 4 3 2 1

Illustrations Credits: NASA / Goddard Space Flight Center Scientific Visualization Studio, p. 17; © 2011 Photos.com, a division of Getty Images. All rights reserved, pp. 1, 3, 4, 6, 8, 9, 13, 14, 20, 22, 24, 27, 29, 30, 31, 33, 34, 35, 36, 37; Shutterstock.com, p. 18; Troy L. Best / Mammal Image Library / American Society of Mammalogists, p. 26.

Cover Illustration: © 2011 Photos.com, a division of Getty Images. All rights reserved (Gray Fox).

CONTENTS

"As far as the eye could see, no trace of vegetation, no plant, not a blade of grass . . . no trace of any animal, no impression from the foot of a living creature in this bare flat ground."[1]

—Scientist Jacob H. Schiel describing the salt flats bordering the Great Salt Lake during the Gunnison-Beckwith expedition (1853-1854). This expedition sought out possible routes for the railroad to the Pacific.

1
EXTREME DESERTS

Exploring the desert is an unforgettable
experience. Most days there is not a cloud to
shade the blazing sun. The air feels extremely dry
and hot, like a heat wave coming out of a burning
oven. Within minutes, any exposed skin shows
signs of sunburn. Even sunlight reflected from the
ground can damage the skin.

The body sweats profusely trying to cool down,
but it's so dry that the water evaporates before it
accumulates on the skin. Precious water abandons
the body in spite of constant lip licking and rapid
blinking to keep the lips and the eyes moist.
Dehydration is a clear threat. If there is water
somewhere, it might be so salty that it's unsafe
to drink.

Spiders are one of many kinds of desert invertebrates.

After a quick search for living creatures, it seems the desert is, well, deserted. Plants are few and far apart. It takes a keen eye to spot a lizard, a rodent, a bird, or an insect. As the sun sets, the temperature drops quickly and the desert becomes more bearable. This is when the desert becomes alive. Careful night explorations reveal a large variety of animals.

Hundreds of animal species live in the desert, big and small. Ants, flies, bees, beetles, butterflies, spiders, scorpions, lizards, snakes, birds, rodents, hares, antelopes, camels, pumas, and coyotes are just some examples of the desert's animals. How do they survive with so little water, the extreme heat, and limited, and sometimes toxic, food supplies?

WHAT IS A DESERT?

A desert is a dry or arid land with few and scattered plants. Deserts are dry because they receive little and irregular rain or snow. What little water does fall from the skies quickly evaporates.

In general, deserts receive about ten inches, or 250 millimeters of rain per year.[2] However, there are areas that receive less than one inch of rain annually. These are the most extreme deserts on Earth. The Atacama Desert in South America is an extremely dry desert; it may not rain there for several years in a row.

Deserts cover about one-fifth of the land area on Earth and are found in Asia, Africa, Australia, North America, and South America. Some people even call the cold, dry, barren regions at the North and South Poles deserts, because they receive only a very small amount of annual precipitation.

MORE THAN DUNES AND HEAT

Many people think that all deserts are large expanses of sand and dunes. About one-fourth of all deserts have large dunes. However, what is more common is ground covered with soil, gravel, or small pebbles. Also located in deserts are dry lakes, or salt pans, where water accumulates briefly during rains and then evaporates leaving a salty crust. There are deserts with tall rock formations sculpted by water and wind while others are surrounded by mountains. Some deserts are at sea level, while others are very high above the sea.

Deserts are known for hot summer days. In the hottest deserts, temperatures may reach 104° Fahrenheit (40° Celsius) or more for many days in a row. But on a winter night, these deserts sometimes reach temperatures below 32°F (0°C). In fact, some deserts have very cold winters where it can even snow.

For example, the Atacama Desert in South America and deserts in Asia are cold. They experience day and night temperatures that are much lower than hot desert temperatures. For example, the Pamir Plateau in Asia has an average temperature of 1.4°F (-17°C), often dropping to -51°F (-46°C) during winter. July is the warmest month with an average temperature of just 57°F (14°C).[3]

Salty rock formations in a pond at Death Valley, which is near the California-Nevada border. The pond is saltier than the ocean.

DESERTS OF THE WORLD (excluding North America)		
HOT DESERTS	**COLD DESERTS**	**LARGEST DESERT**
Sahara, Arabian, Kalahari, and Great Victoria	Gobi, Atacama, and Namib	Sahara: It's about 2.9 million square miles (7.4 million square kilometers), nearly one-fourth of the African continent.[4]

NORTH AMERICAN DESERTS				
DESERT	**LOCATION**	**SIZE (mi² / km²)**	**CHARACTERISTICS**	**SOME ANIMALS**
Chihuahuan	North Central Mexico and Southwestern USA (Arizona, New Mexico, Texas)	175,700 / 455,000	Hot desert: High elevation with rocky areas, many mountains and mesas.	Coyote, diamondback rattlesnake, javelin, kangaroo rat, roadrunner
Great Basin	Western USA (Idaho, Nevada, Oregon, Utah, and California)	190,000 / 492,100	Cold desert: Many mountains, basins (land draining into a lake or rivers) and large salt flats.	Bighorn sheep, jackrabbit, pocket mouse, antelope, lizards
Sonoran	Baja Peninsula of Mexico and Southwestern USA (Arizona and California)	120,500 / 312,000	Hot desert: Sandy soil and gravel.	Elf owl, **gila monster**, kangaroo rat, pack rat, roadrunner, sidewinder rattlesnake, tarantula
Mojave	Southwestern USA (Arizona, California, Nevada, and Utah)	25,100 / 65,000	Hot desert: Sandy soil, gravel, and salt flats.	Bighorn sheep, coyote, jackrabbit, sidewinder rattlesnake, zebra-tailed lizard

THE HOTTEST AND COLDEST PLACES ON EARTH ARE DESERTS

Weather stations around the world measure the air temperature. The highest air temperature ever recorded is 136°F (57.8°C) in the desert of El Azizia, Libya, on September 13, 1922.[5] The lowest temperature ever recorded is -132°F (-91°C) at the Russian research station at Vostok, Antarctica, in 1997.

WATER IN THE DESERT

Desert creatures are challenged by very limited water supply, extreme heat, bright sun, and often strong winds. Deserts receive very little rain because the air carries little moisture.

When it does rain, it may be for a few days or weeks in a year. Water accumulates in ponds, flat lakes, or creeks. Part of the water seeps underground. It might be stored deep beneath the ground in large deposits. Sometimes rain may be torrential, and the land does not have time to absorb it. Water may run off carrying rocks, soil, and other materials with it. Desert plants and animals have learned to live with the limited water supply. It is during these brief periods of precipitation that plants bloom—sometimes painting deserts with rainbow colors—and animals have their young.

WHY DO DESERTS HAVE EXTREME TEMPERATURES?

The dry air contributes to the intense hot days and cold nights. Moisture in the air absorbs or deflects the sun's radiation. But dry air lets much of the sun's rays reach the ground and heats it intensely. At night, the warmth of the desert escapes easily through the dry air into space, and the temperature drops significantly.

Low moisture and heat feed back on each other. Heat increases evaporation, which dries the land, and the lack of moisture in the air allows more sunlight to pass through it and heat the ground.

WHY ARE DESERTS WINDY?

Strong winds and sandstorms are common in the desert. Winds occur because the hot ground warms up the air. As the hot air rises, colder air flows down to take its place. This creates winds that may be fast and strong and create dust or sandstorms. Strong winds limit the time animals have to look for food or water. Wind is one force shaping the desert. The dust it carries can travel a long distance and is often carried out of the desert. Sand, on the other hand, is heavier and cannot be carried as far. Wind can carry it across open lands, but, as the wind slows near mountains or other obstacles, the sand falls and can form large dunes.

2

TYPES OF DESERTS

Deserts form for various reasons that cause little precipitation and high evaporation.[1]

SUBTROPICAL DESERTS

Most of the world's deserts are located just north or south of the Earth's equator. They form because dry, hot air is constantly present in those areas. This is how this happens.

The air around the Earth circulates constantly in a complex manner. As air masses flow around the Earth, they warm up or cool down and change the amount of moisture they carry. The area around the equator receives most of the solar radiation of the planet, which keeps the air very warm. The air also carries a lot of moisture, or water vapor, because the intense warmth evaporates large amounts of water from the oceans.

Warm air rises. As it rises in the sky, it slowly cools, which causes the moisture to condense and rain to fall, making the tropics wet. After this rain falls, the air is depleted of moisture and winds carry this dry air to regions north and south of the equator. The presence of these hot, dry air masses results in the formation of some of the most extreme deserts on Earth, such as the Sahara and the deserts of Australia and southern Africa.

A view of the Australian desert.

The Atacama Desert in South America is a cold desert.

BIODIVERSITY IN THE DESERT

In spite of the extreme environmental conditions, the desert is rich in animal and plant life. Michael Mares compared the number of species of mammals living in the Amazon rain forest and in the drylands of South America. He found that the drylands are the richest area, supporting a larger number of species of very different kinds. Many of these animals live in deserts only. Deserts should be preserved as much as the Amazonian rain forest and other ecosystems of our planet.[2]

RAIN SHADOW DESERTS

Rain shadow deserts form on the downwind, or leeward, side of a mountain range. The mountains act as an enormous barrier preventing moisture from reaching the leeward side.

The Great Basin Desert of North America, for instance, is located on the eastern or leeward slope of the Sierra Nevada and Cascade mountains. Warm, moist air flowing inland from the Pacific Ocean flows upward as it meets the western side of the mountain. The rising air cools and the moisture condenses and falls either as rain or snow.

COOL COASTAL DESERTS

There are deserts that form very close to the coast, bordering cold oceans. The ocean is so cold that little water evaporates and dry air reaches the land.

Some of the driest deserts are cool, coastal deserts, such as the Atacama Desert in South America and the Namib Desert of western Africa. Sections of the desert of Baja California in North America are deserts because they border the cold California current.[3] The little moisture that cold, coastal deserts receive comes in the form of fog that moves inland from the open ocean.

CONTINENTAL DESERTS

Deserts may also form at the very center of large continents. The Gobi Desert of central Asia is so far away from the coast that by the time ocean winds reach the region, they have lost their moisture. Some parts of the Australian Desert are also formed this way.

3
HOW DESERTS HAPPENED

A long, long time ago, today's deserts did not exist. About 60 million years ago in North America, for example, the land occupied now by the Great Basin, the Mojave, the Chihuahuan, and the Sonoran deserts supported forests and woodlands. Temperatures were not extreme, and it rained regularly and abundantly. In consequence, many types of plants grew, and many types of animals thrived. But in time, this moist environment became an arid land.[1]

This happened because the earth is dynamic—it changes over the years, millions of years. The continents drift because they are resting on tectonic plates. These are gigantic segments of the Earth's crust carried by magma, or lava, flowing underneath, like rafts slowly carried by ocean currents.

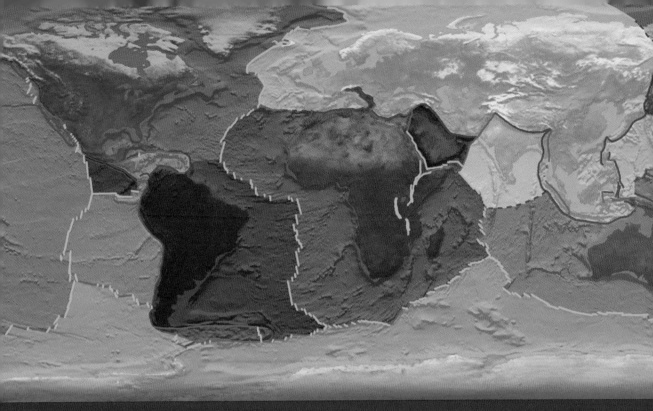

The different colors illustrate how Earth's crust is divided into tectonic plates.

Tectonic plates may collide and slowly push against each other or one may slide under the other. The force of the collision may be huge and cause mountains to grow or parts of the seafloor to rise to the surface (that's why people find seashells in rocks on the top of mountains). Weather patterns change and the oceans cool down and warm up. These phenomena have been transforming the Earth for millions of years. In North America, the uplift of the Sierra Nevada and the Rocky mountains and the Sierra Madre of Mexico, created a rain-shadow effect that led to the formation of deserts. The mountains blocked moist-laden clouds coming from the Pacific Ocean and the Gulf of Mexico. The clouds dropped their moisture on the ocean side of the mountains and the deserts developed on the dry side.[2]

The Sahara Desert has gone through many climate changes throughout history. This is a view of the Sahara in Tadrart, Algeria.

THE CHANGING SAHARA

About 3 million years ago, the land occupied by the Sahara Desert was under the ocean. Scientists know this because they have found whalebones, seashells, and the remains of other aquatic creatures under the sand. The Sahara came to the surface because tectonic plates in the Earth's crust moved and lifted the land above the sea.

Since then, North Africa has gone through a series of dry and wet phases. When the Sahara receives less radiation and more rain, a tropical environment develops.[3] More radiation and less rain, promotes the transformation into a desert, which may take two hundred years. About two thousand years ago, during the rule of the Roman Empire, Tunisia, which is now 76 percent desert, was humid and a major provider of agricultural products.[4] Deserts change over time, and this means that plants and animals have to adapt to the changing conditions to survive.

The continent of Antarctica slowly moved south to its current position. The land began to accumulate snow and the oceans around it began to freeze. The world's oceans progressively chilled, air temperatures dropped, and precipitation decreased inland. In North America, these changes caused forests and woodlands to retreat into bordering mountains with more moisture. Some plants became extinct when they could not adapt to living with less water and lowering temperatures. Little by little, the North American deserts formed.[5]

The animals that lived in these areas also had to move or adapt if they were to survive in the growing desert. The descendants of those that adapted populate the deserts today. These animal species have learned to live with little water, extreme temperatures, and limited food sources. These are among the most extreme challenges for living creatures.

4
LIVING IN AN ARID LAND

Even though extreme temperatures and limited food pose important challenges to desert animals, it is the lack of water that really challenges their ability to survive.[1]

As deserts were forming, animals and plants faced an environment that progressively provided less and less water. Animals are 60 to 80 percent water by weight. Survival became a matter of finding new sources of moisture and avoiding losing body fluids. This is how animals have conquered extreme deserts.

The desert locusts of North Africa can form swarms that travel great distances.

CHANGING THEIR BEHAVIOR

Some animals adapted to the drier land by traveling long distances to find water. There are birds in the southern American deserts, like the white-winged dove, that must look for water twice a day. They drink large amounts and may increase their weight by more than 15 percent.

Large mammals, such as camels in Africa and Asia, can walk for days without drinking. When they find water, they drink huge amounts—think of drinking thirty one-gallon-milk jugs, quickly. Bighorn sheep move away from their watering hole looking for food, and they return to drink every three to five days. Feral burros can survive for a week without drinking and, like the camel, will drink profusely when they find water. If coyotes do not find surface water, they dig a hole up to 3.3 feet (1 meter) deep in sandy areas around creeks.

Animals that do not travel long distances, such as nonflying insects and spiders, reptiles, and small mammals, have adapted by living without drinking much water or none at all. The tenebrionid beetle of the Namib Desert obtains water from the fog that enters the desert from the ocean. The beetle faces the fog with its head down. The water condenses on its body and runs down to its mouth. The body surface of some adult insects and larvae can absorb water from the humid air.[2]

The desert cockroach of the Sonoran Desert digs into the sand where the humidity is about 80 percent. Then it extends two pouches covered with moisture-absorbing hairs out from its mouth. Water droplets stick to the hairs and accumulate in the pouches.

Dromedary, or one-humped, camels of the Sahara Desert originated in North America.

GETTING WATER FROM FOODS AND METABOLISM

Most desert animals do not need to drink water at all. They get enough water from the foods they eat and from their metabolism (chemical reactions within their bodies).

Roadrunners can live on a diet of mice alone. They absorb the water in the mice's body and produce water when they digest it.

The white-tailed antelope ground squirrel can live without drinking water by eating crickets.

Having a flexible diet goes a long way for desert animals. The black-throated sparrow gets enough water in the spring eating leaves, nectar, and insects. When it gets drier, the sparrow eats seeds and must drink from water holes.

Merriam's kangaroo rat does not drink water. It survives on a diet of seeds alone, which are about 10 percent water in weight. This amazing little rodent collects large amounts of seeds and stores them in underground burrows, which are more humid than the surface. The seeds absorb the humidity, which mostly comes from the moisture kangaroo rats breathe out. In this way, stored seeds may raise their water content to 20 percent. This strategy allows the kangaroo rat to get enough moisture from seeds without having to drink. It also recycles some of the moisture it breathes out, reducing the amount of water lost.[3]

BALANCING WATER LOSS

In the desert, saving water is as important as obtaining water. The desert air "is like a sponge drawing water out of an animal. In fact, the evaporative water loss from an animal is driven by the humidity of the air; the drier the air, the greater the rate of evaporation."[4]

LOSING WATER FROM THE SURFACE

Some animals reduce water loss by using protective covers or moving to more humid spots, such as areas underground. Insects and spiders have a hard covering coated with waxy materials that decrease water loss. The desert scorpion of the Sonoran Desert changes its covering with the seasons. During summer, the chemical composition reduces evaporation. During the winter, when temperatures and humidity are milder, the

Fennec foxes are so well adapted to desert conditions that they do not have to drink water to survive.

GAINING AND LOSING WATER IN THE DESERT

Desert animals gain water by:
- drinking
- ingesting it with prey and plants
- generating water through their body's metabolic reactions

Desert animals lose water in various ways:
- from their respiratory tract when they breathe out (breath is very humid)
- from their skin or shell
- from the feces and urine
- from materials they regurgitate, or throw up
- from water in milk or in eggs
- from defense secretions some animals squirt to protect themselves from predators.

chemical composition changes to make the covering more permeable. Reptiles' skin, not the scales, reduces water loss.

Amphibians do not drink. They obtain and lose water through the skin. The hotter and drier the environment, the more they lose. This is a tremendous challenge for amphibians. Frogs and toads, such as the spadefoot toad of the southern American deserts, survive dry periods by waiting for rain underground. They dig deep holes searching for moist soil and stay in a sleeplike state until the rain returns. Sometimes they wait for two years or more, enveloped in a cocoon to control water loss. Even in this protected state, the spadefoot may lose 50 percent of its water and still survive.[5]

When it rains and water accumulates on the surface, toads and frogs emerge from their sleep. This water will probably evaporate in a few weeks, so there is little time to produce the next generation.

These amphibians lay eggs that develop into adults faster than frogs living in humid environments.

Birds' and mammals' skins are several times more permeable than reptile skin. Fur and feathers provide extra protection against evaporation. There are mammals, such as the cactus mouse, however, whose skin is as impermeable as that of reptiles.

LOSING WATER WHEN BREATHING, IN URINE, AND IN FECES

Animals lose water through moist internal surfaces, such as their lungs as they breathe. However, in some desert animals, the nose recovers about 70 percent of the moisture before the air is exhaled. The nose is cooler than the air coming from the lungs. The air cools down as it passes through the nose and moisture condenses.

Kangaroo rats of North American deserts usually spend the daytime inside shallow burrows with openings near the bases of shrubs.

Animals lose water in urine. All animals urinate to discard body waste. One of the main waste materials is ammonia, which is very toxic and needs a lot of water to eliminate it. Desert animals save water by transforming ammonia into urea, which is less toxic. It needs half the amount of water that ammonia needs to be discarded. Mammals and adult amphibians produce urea.

Insects, reptiles, and birds produce uric acid, which saves the most water because it is eliminated as crystals.[6]

Toads and frogs have big bladders that can hold urine up to 50 percent of their body weight. They recycle water from this urine to stay moist during dry periods. Tortoises also have big bladders and recycle water from the urine.

Animals lose water in their feces because the waste is usually very moist—more than 75 percent water. Desert animals recycle this water as the feces pass through the gut before eliminating them. Insects and spiders are very good at drying their waste, and they produce dry pellets. The Great Basin pocket mouse produces feces that are 36 percent water. These are among the driest feces among mammals.

Scorpions of the Mojave Desert hide under rocks to avoid extreme heat.

5
LIVING IN THE HEAT

Animals must have a particular body temperature to live, and if they are too cold or too warm, they are unable to move, drink, or digest food. Animals are ectotherms (cold-blooded) or endotherms (warm-blooded) depending on how they adjust their body temperature. Ectotherms depend on their environment to adjust their body temperature. Endotherms, on the other hand, produce their own heat inside their bodies. Both groups are very successful in the desert, but ectotherms are the most abundant and varied group. Ectotherms and endotherms have several adapting behaviors that allow them to survive the harsh desert climates.

STAYING OUT OF THE HEAT

Many animals in the desert avoid the sun during the day and come out at night when it is cooler. They spend the day under rocks or plants that provide shade. Underground, however, is the preferred hiding location. Many insects, spiders, scorpions, amphibians, reptiles, and mammals dig burrows.

THE GRAY FOX

The gray fox feels at home in the desert. Its color blends well with its surroundings, providing camouflage. It stays away from the heat and the dry weather by sheltering in underground burrows during the day and emerging at dusk to find food when it is cooler. The gray fox can dig for water when necessary. It also has flexible eating habits—it is an omnivore. During fall and winter, it eats fruits from trees and shrubs, as well as gophers, mice, and carrion. In the summer, when there are no more fruits and berries, the gray fox eats insects. There is one thing that separates this relative of the dog from the other foxes: It can climb trees and jump from branch to branch. It helps that it is about the size of a small dog. Climbing trees is useful for both finding food and to evade predators, such as golden eagles, coyotes, and humans.

When it is time to find food, the North American gray fox keeps its cubs in underground burrows to protect them from the extreme heat as well as predators.

THE COOLEST PLACE IN THE DESERT

During the day, underground is several degrees cooler than the surface—the deeper, the cooler. It is also more humid. Living underground is more common in deserts than in less extreme areas.

Animals dig at different depths. Most burrows are between 8 inches (20 centimeters) and 28 inches (70 centimeters) deep. Rodents can dig deeper than 3.3 feet (1 meter) and ants even deeper, to 6.6 feet (2 meters) underground. Burrowing animals close the burrow's entrance to keep it cool and moist.

The burrowing owl feeds on animals that dig burrows in open areas, such as spiders and small mammals. It is small in size and can mimic the sound of a rattlesnake.

Living underground has more advantages. It provides a hiding place against predators, access to food such as roots and worms, and a place to store food and to hide young away from the extreme environment.[1]

BASKING IN THE SUN

Ectotherms regulate their body temperature mainly by their behavior. The desert iguana is a good example. Iguanas are large lizards that spend the night in burrows or under rocks, which are several degrees warmer than the cool open surface. Their body temperature decreases through the night. But when the sun rises, lizards come out and bask in the sun. They may lay their bodies flat on a warm rock. Or they can warm up fast by placing their body broadside facing the sun. Heat transfers from the warm surface to the lizard's skin. Blood rushes to the skin and warms up, which in turn warms the organs inside.

The collared peccary, or javelina, is not related to the pig despite its resemblance. Its habitat includes the Chihuahuan and Sonoran deserts. It is active in the early morning and at dusk. One of its favorite fruits is the prickly pear cactus. It is named the javelina because of its razor-sharp tusks. *Javelina* is derived from *jabalina*, the Spanish word for javelin or spear.

As the body warms up, the iguana can move quicker to find food, evade predators, or lay eggs.

As the day heats up and the iguana begins to overheat, it moves to a cooler location. Again blood rushes to the skin, but this time it is to give body heat to the cool ground or air in the shade. If the iguana cools down too much, it moves back to a warmer surface. If the iguana overheats, it can pant to cool down. Panting, however, spends water and iguanas only do it as a last resort.

When the white-tailed antelope ground squirrel overheats, it cools down fast by extending its legs and laying its belly flat on cool rocks or ground. This can drop the squirrel's temperature more than one degree per minute. The squirrel also uses its tail to shade its body.

POSTURES AND LOCOMOTION

Lizards, snakes, insects, and some mammals cool down by assuming various postures or with unique locomotion. Lizards minimize heating by lifting one or two feet at a time from the hot sand. In this way, they gain up to half the heat gained by keeping all feet on the ground. Sidewinder rattlesnakes of North American deserts and the sidewinding adder of the Namib African desert slither through hot dunes in a unique way that minimizes contact with the surface.

Insects cool down by standing above the ground, as if on stilts. The separation from the hot surface cools them down as air flows underneath. Lizards and insects stand tall parallel to the sun's rays to minimize the amount of radiation received.

SLEEPING IT OUT

The pocket mouse of the Mojave Desert can spend winter in torpor, or a sleeplike state, to avoid cold temperatures and limited food. The mouse hides in a burrow and reduces its body temperature near the burrow's temperature, as low as 34°F (1°C). This reduces the metabolic rate to about 4 percent of its normal rate, saving energy.

The mouse may spend about five months in torpor. It alternates between periods of sleep and activity until the weather becomes warmer and food more abundant. Torpor in winter is sometimes called hibernation when the animal does not awake at all until the surface conditions are better. The pocket mouse may also pass summer in torpor underground, avoiding the hot environment on the surface.

USING COLOR

Some lizards change their skin color to vary heat absorption. The desert iguana of the Mojave and Sonoran deserts is black in the morning, which helps it warm up, absorbing the sunlight it receives. As its temperature rises, its color lightens. If the temperature continues to rise, the iguana becomes white. This color absorbs little sunlight and reduces the chances of overheating.

The roadrunner warms up by exposing its black feathers to the sun.

The roadrunner saves energy by lowering its body temperature at night. It warms up in the morning by raising its back feathers and exposing the black skin underneath to the morning sun. The black skin absorbs sunlight, which warms up the roadrunner.

TAKING THE HEAT

Insects and scorpions are among the toughest desert animals. Some ants can tolerate very high temperatures—up to 126°F (52°C)—that would kill other animals. Ants can explore the land under the scorching desert looking for animals that gave in to the heat. Desert cicadas can still sing at temperatures up to 117°F (47°C) when their predators hide from the heat. Camels, the addax antelope, and some rodents also tolerate very high body temperatures.[2]

LONG EARS AND LEGS

Many desert animals have long legs or long ears covered with a thin layer of feathers or fur. Some have both. Think of the long legs of camels, desert flamingoes, jackrabbits, kangaroo rats, jerboas from the Sahara

The light-colored fur of the addax antelope helps it stay cool in the Sahara Desert.

The jackrabbit uses its long ears to cool down.

The emu of the Australian Desert uses its long, featherless legs to cool itself.

(which look very similar to the kangaroo rats of North American deserts), Australian kangaroos, and other mammals that jump. The jackrabbit, the fennec fox of the Sahara, and the kit fox of the North American deserts have long ears.

When warm blood flows in vessels along the surface of long, exposed legs and ears, they release heat to the air around it. When they need to keep warm, these animals bend their long ears or legs under their body reducing heat loss.

COOLING WITH WATER

One of the most effective ways to cool down is by evaporating a liquid on the body surface—called evaporative cooling. This cools down the body because heat is used to evaporate the liquid. The downside of evaporative cooling in the desert is that it uses a lot of water that would need to be replaced.

Sweating is not common in desert animals. It is usually used when other strategies do not prevent overheating. Reptiles cool down by panting. Tortoises and turtles urinate on themselves or spread saliva on their body. The white-tailed antelope ground squirrel produces huge amounts of saliva that it spreads on its neck and chest. Given the chance, animals cool down quickly by dipping in water pools.

RATTLESNAKES

Slithering along the hot desert, rattlesnakes are one of the most impressive desert animals. Like other cold-blooded desert dwellers, rattlesnakes combine a variety of strategies to survive extreme conditions. The way they move on the scorching ground minimizes the amount of heat they receive. Some have light colors or patterns that work as camouflage. They stay cool and save water by hiding during the day in burrows and under rocks. They get water from their food. They hunt at night using their smell and heat sensors to find prey. They warn predators and try to impress prey by rattling their tails. When they shake their tail, adjacent rattle segments rub against each other producing a rattling sound. Their rattle gains a new segment each time they shed their skin. This may happen two or more times every year. Never underestimate a rattlesnake. All of them are poisonous and capture their prey or defend themselves by injecting deadly venom with their fangs.[3]

The western diamondback rattlesnake lives in the Chihuahuan Desert of North America. It hunts by following scent trails and detecting the heat produced by its prey. Notice its rattle (at bottom), which it uses to warn other animals to stay away.

6
FOOD CHALLENGES

Desert animals eat a variety of animal and plant foods offered by the desert looking for nutrients and water. However, some animals have adapted by eating toxic foods often ignored by most animals.

The saltbush has green, water- and nutrient-rich leaves all year long, but it is extremely salty. This plant absorbs the abundant, salty underground water found around salt pans. The saltbush deposits salt on the surface of leaves, like a white crust. Eating too much salt is toxic, so most herbivores do not eat this plant. However, the chisel-toothed kangaroo rat is not discouraged at all.

Kangaroo rats hold saltbush leaves with their forefeet (hands) and scrape away all the salt by passing the leaf over the lower incisors about ten times. Then they turn the leaf over and repeat the process, which all together takes about twenty seconds. The sharp teeth look like a chisel, which is a cutting tool with a flat, beveled or slanted blade.

Interestingly, two other unrelated rodents from distant deserts have similar adaptations. The fat sand rat of the Sahara in Africa also uses its lower incisors to scrape salt away. In the Monte Desert of South America, the red vizcaya rat uses its lower incisors and two "bristle bundles" of hard hairs that vibrate to scrape the salt away. Using bristles in addition to the lower incisors helps this animal remove all the salt in about two seconds, eating many leaves in the time the kangaroo rat cleans up one. These rodents also have special kidneys that filter excess salt out.[1]

Desert animals are amazing creatures that have conquered one of the most challenging environments on the planet. Their flexible behaviors and numerous strategies to survive in the desert are magnificent examples of the wonders of the animal world.

HANDS-ON ACTIVITY
THE COOLING POWER OF SHADE

Many desert animals avoid losing excessive water by staying under shade. Test the effect of shade on evaporation with this simple experiment.

MATERIALS

- 2 bowls of the same size and shape
- water
- marker
- two thermometers

PROCEDURE

1. Fill each bowl with the same amount of water at room temperature, close to the rim.

2. Mark the water level with the marker.

3. Place one of the bowls under direct sun and mark it "Sun." Place the other bowl nearby under shade (such as a tree or wide bush) and mark it "Shade." (Make sure the second bowl stays under shade for the entire experiment.)

4. Alternatively, do this experiment indoors placing the "Sun" bowl under a desk lamp with a 100 Watt light bulb. Place the "Shade' bowl nearby but covered with shade.

WATER TEMPERATURE (°F or °C)							
TIME	**0**	**1**	**2**	**3**	**4**	**5**	**6**
SUN							
SHADE							

5. Measure the initial water temperature (Time 0) on each bowl and write it in the table (see above).

6. Measure the temperature of the water in each bowl every thirty minutes and write it in the table. Every thirty minutes, mark the water level in each bowl.

REACH YOUR CONCLUSIONS

1. Which bowl lost the most water?

2. Which water warmed up the most?

3. What would happen if you placed a piece of wax paper right on top of the water in the "Sun" bowl before placing the bowl under the sun? Would more or less water evaporate? Check it out!

CHAPTER NOTES

Chapter 1. Extreme Deserts

1. Jacob H. Schiel, *Journey Through the Rocky Mountains and the Humboldt Mountains to the Pacific Ocean,* trans. and ed. Thomas N. Bonner (Norman, Okla.: University of Oklahoma Press, 1959), p. 114. Scientist Jacob H. Schiel describes the salt flats bordering the Great Salt Lake during the Gunnison-Beckwith expedition (1853–1854). This expedition sought out possible routes for the railroad to the Pacific.
2. Michael M. Mares, *Encyclopedia of Deserts* (Norman, Okla.: University of Oklahoma Press, 1999), p. xxx.
3. Ibid., p. 48.
4. Ibid., p. 488.
5. D. J. Mildrexier, M. Zhao, and S. W. Running, "Where Are the Hottest Spots on Earth?" *EOS,* vol. 87, no. 43, October 26, 2006, pp. 461–467, <http://earthobservatory.nasa.gov/IOTD/view.php?id=7149> (January 17, 2010).

Chapter 2. Types of Deserts

1. John Sowell, *Desert Ecology: An Introduction to Life in the Arid Southwest* (Salt Lake City, Utah: University of Utah Press, 2001), pp. 3–17.
2. Michael A. Mares, "Neotropical Mammals and the Myth of Amazonian Biodiversity," *Science,* vol. 255, 1992, pp. 976–977.
3. S. D. Bradshaw, *Ecophysiology of Desert Reptiles* (North Ryde, New South Wales, Australia: Academic Press Australia, 1986), p. 13.

Chapter 3. How Deserts Happened

1. S. D. Bradshaw, *Ecophysiology of Desert Reptiles* (North Ryde, New South Wales, Australia: Academic Press Australia, 1986), p. 38.
2. D. I. Axelrod, "Paleobotanical History of the Western Deserts," *The Origin and Evolution of Deserts,* ed. Stephen G. Wells and Donald R. Haragan (Albuquerque, N. Mex: University of New Mexico Press, 1983), p. 115.

3. P. B. deMenocal, "Africa on the Edge," *Nature Geoscience*, vol. 1, October 2008, p. 650.
4. Bradshaw, p. 22.
5. Axelrod, p. 116.

Chapter 4. Living in an Arid Land

1. John Sowell, *Desert Ecology: An Introduction to Life in the Arid Southwest* (Salt Lake City, Utah: University of Utah Press, 2001), p. 81.
2. Ibid., p. 84.
3. Michael A. Mares, *Desert Calling: Life in a Forbidding Landscape* (Boston: Harvard University Press, 2002), p. 29.
4. Sowell, p. 87
5. Michael M. Mares, *Encyclopedia of Deserts* (Norman, Okla.: University of Oklahoma Press, 1999), p. 21.
6. Ibid., p. 324.

Chapter 5. Living in the Heat

1. John Sowell, *Desert Ecology: An Introduction to Life in the Arid Southwest* (Salt Lake City, Utah: University of Utah Press, 2001), p. 69.
2. Michael M. Mares, *Encyclopedia of Deserts* (Norman, Okla.: University of Oklahoma Press, 1999), p. 96.
3. Ibid., p. 467.

Chapter 6. Food Challenges

1. M. A. Mares et al., "How Desert Rodents Overcome Halophytic Plant Defenses," *BioScience*, vol. 47, no. 10, 1997, pp. 699–704.

GLOSSARY

AMPHIBIAN • A cold-blooded animal with smooth skin, such as a frog, that can live both on land and in water.

ARID • Dry.

DEHYDRATION • A lack of water in the body.

ECOSYSTEM • A group of organisms, their environment, and the relationships among them.

ECTOTHERM • An animal that maintains its body temperature by absorbing heat from the environment.

ENDOTHERM • An animal that keeps its body temperature constant despite temperature changes in the environment.

HIBERNATION • A state of reduced activity that helps an animal survive the winter.

HYDRATE • To provide water to reestablish water balance.

LEEWARD • Away from the wind.

MAMMAL • A warm-blooded animal that has its skin covered by hair and feeds its young with milk.

METABOLISM • Body chemical reactions that transform food into energy needed to support life.

REPTILE • A cold-blooded animal with scales or hard plates on its skin, such as snakes, lizards, crocodiles, and turtles.

SALT PAN • Flat ground covered with a crust of salt.

TECTONIC PLATES • Segments of the Earth's crust that drift carried by magma.

TORPOR • A state of reduced activity that helps animals survive extreme environmental conditions.

FURTHER READING

Books

Ceceri, Kathryn. *Discover the Desert: The Driest Place on Earth.* White River Junction, Vt.: Nomad Press, 2009.

Lundgren, Julie K. *Desert Dinners: Studying Food Webs in the Desert.* Vero Beach, Fla.: Rourke Pub., 2009.

Munro, Roxie. *Desert Days, Desert Nights.* Houston, Tex.: Bright Sky Press, 2010.

Wiewandt, Thomas. *Hidden Life of the Desert.* Missoula, Mont.: Mountain Press Publishing Company, 2010.

Internet Addresses

Desert Animals

<http://www.desertanimals.net/>

Desert USA: Exploring the Southwest

<http://www.desertusa.com/index.html>

MBGnet: Biomes of the World—Desert

<http://www.mbgnet.net/sets/desert/index.htm>

Ana María Rodríguez's Homepage

<http://www.anamariarodriguez.com>

INDEX